Contributors

David Seaburn
Don Young
DR Susannah Ward
Ken Steele
Michael Kornbluth
Candace MacPhie
J. M. Shaw
Jonni Jordyn
Luce Sutherland
Angela Van Breemen
Zane Carson Carruth
Brad C. Anderson
Don Sawyer
Dr. Katherine Hutchinson-Hayes
José Orlando Castañeda
Alexander Ellis

Review Tales
A Book Magazine For Indie Authors

Founder & Editor in Chief: S. Jeyran Main
Publisher: Review Tales Publishing & Editing Services
Print & Distribution: Ingram Spark
Designs: Pexels
ISBN 978-1-988680-62-0 (Paperback)
ISBN 978-1-988680-63-7 (Digital)
www.jeyranmain.com
For all inquiries, please contact us directly.

Photo Credits from Pexels:
ioanamtc-4346281
polina-kovaleva-6954751
polina-kovaleva-6965701
polina-zimmerman-3747468

Editor's Note

Dear Readers,

Welcome to the 14th issue of Review Tales, a special edition brimming with wisdom and insight from some of the most talented voices in the literary world. As always, our aim is to share the untold stories and behind-the-scenes moments that shape a writer's journey, offering you a glimpse into the heart and soul of the creative process.

This issue features thought-provoking articles like In Defence of Language by David Seaburn, where he champions the power of words and the craft of writing in an age where language is constantly evolving. Don Young reminds us that It's a Fine Time to Be a Writer, offering a fresh perspective on the opportunities that come with today's publishing landscape. Meanwhile, Dr. Susannah Ward guides us in Mastering Real Wellness, showing how writers can maintain balance in their lives while nurturing creativity. Ken Steele's The Promise of Unbroken Straw explores the profound impact of storytelling on both the writer and reader, leaving us with a renewed sense of purpose.

We are also thrilled to bring you exclusive interviews, author confessions, and editor's picks that will inspire, teach, and perhaps even surprise you with what happens behind the pages.

As always, we are proud to provide a platform for these incredible voices, whose stories not only enrich the literary world but also encourage fellow writers to continue pushing boundaries. We hope you enjoy this issue and find inspiration within its pages.

Happy reading,

Jeyran Main

Editor-in-Chief
Review Tales Magazine

SPRING 2025 | ISSUE 14

Contents

In Defense of Language
David Seaburn

I have been writing novels for twenty-four years. My tenth novel, Until It Was Gone, was released recently, and my eleventh is in (endless) revision. A great many changes have occurred since I first started writing stories. Among the most disconcerting (since I am a writer) has been the degradation of language and how it is now used more often to confuse, mislead, and manipulate than to clarify, enlighten, and inspire, to create shadows rather than cast light.

It has been such a persistent and pervasive phenomenon that, at times, I have feared I might slip into a numbed cynical acceptance that this is the way it is, that I can no longer trust language to make sense. Since I am a writer, this is more than a little discomfiting.

In an interview on the podcast Writers on Writing, the author, George Saunders, was asked to comment on the place of writing and art today when so much in our society seems to be falling apart. Saunders, a fiction writer, had done research during the recent presidential campaign for a magazine article, research that included attending many Trump rallies. I anticipated that Saunders would beat the social action drum, which he acknowledged was a viable option. Instead, he suggested that writing at a high level may be more critical now than ever before. He noted how much communication has become degrading, combative, crude, and abusive. He suggested the writing was necessary "if only to remind ourselves as a species that a high mode of communication is possible." He said we should "keep a sacred chapel where... making models of the world that are intricate, faithful and loving" still exists.

I found his thoughts heartening.

I write to use language to elucidate what it means to be a plain old human living in the world. That is my "sacred chapel." I want to lift what seems familiar so it can be seen for its uncommon complexity and beauty. To do this, I must handle letters, words, sentences, and paragraphs respectfully because they are all I have; they are my lenses, ciphers, and pavers; they are the only means I have for making sense of the world and wringing meaning from it. If I become lazy, no longer care how I use it, or lose respect for language, everything is lost. I am left to muddle through vast plains of verbiage devoid of sense, language no longer in the service of meaningful expression, human connection, or even the most straightforward exchange of accurate information. I know there are many ways to change the world, to affect the lives of others, and to elevate the well-being of the many, and they are all important. But for now, I will be a defender of language, someone who endeavors to write in "intricate and faithful and loving ways."

Its a Fine Time To Be a Writer

Don Young

A few weeks ago, I had the wonderful experience of holding my first novel, THE 4MIDABLES -How They Came to Be. After years of writing scripts—and being very fortunate to have several make it onto TV screens—holding "Author's Copy" had me reflecting on my long journey that began when there were only three US TV networks and "store" ming" was still many years away.

In early 1983, my Los Angeles agent set up a meeting for me in Toronto with a producer from France who had created a goofy character with some gadgets. He could have hired more experienced writers but must have sensed Inspector Gadget might become a huge hit, which meant paying Guild writers residuals for years. I had just earned my first writing credit for a TV movie and needed one more to join the Guild, so I was hired along with eleven writers.

E-mail wasn't a thing yet, so the story editor dispatched a taxi to my home with three pages of the storyline in an envelope. I typed the teleplay on me. Please wait for it. It's a Smith Corona electric typewriter! Computers? Those were still a few years away. Four days and 34 pages later, a taxi would arrive to pick up my precious pages and hand me a new "0" x "3". After we finished, the producer offered me a full-time position in Los Angeles, so I headed west, seeking fame and fortune.

Unfortunately, immigration had other ideas, such as refusing to grant a visa to a young Canadian who would take a job from a US writer. I've read many great screenplays over the years and optioned a few with partners to try to get them produced. Unfortunately, we failed, and these wonderful stories created by talented writers were consigned to a hard drive in a drawer instead of being a pleasant memory for millions of people. I made THE 4MIDABLES in 2007 as a cartoon series, and a year later, it was so close to being "green-lit" when the deal collapsed. I put it on the shelf, knowing I would come back at some point to breathe new life into it.

Sixteen years later, I saw how colossal self-publishing had become and realized it might be possible to build a small 'fan base' of several hundred (a few thousand?) loyal readers to provide "social proof" so Disney and Netflix might agree with me on its potential as a live-action Series. Some writers of those great screenplays may turn their stories into a paperback and e-book on Amazon. Producers are always seeking great stories, and with self-publishing booming, the opportunities have never been more plentiful for writers. It's not that many years ago where that just wasn't an option. Forty-one years ago, typing a "Gadget" episode on my Smith Corona, if Michael J. Fox had loaned me his Delorean to go to the future instead, I would have been very bewildered seeing the seismic changes coming to media delivery. Self-publish a novel digitally? Connect with millions of potential readers in multiple countries via 'social networks'? People will read books on a screen called a 'tablet'. Buy a paperback in a store you can't walk inside? It's all happened, and I can't imagine what even the next ten years will bring! That's why now is a fine time to be a writer! Good luck! Never stop creating! Be well!

THE4MIDABLES

How They Came To Be

Mastering Real Wellness
by DR Susannah Ward

A self-mastery framework to create holistic health and optimal living

Mastering Real Wellness

DR SUSANNAH WARD
Specialist Rehabilitation Medicine
BMedSci (Hons) MBBS (Hons) FAFRM RYT® 200

When did you first realize you wanted to be a writer?

I was laser-focused on becoming a doctor from a young age, but the idea to write Mastering Real Wellness struck in my late 20s, during a personal health and well-being crisis as a junior doctor. I'd achieved my dreams but felt stuck, lost, and craving more control over my life. Fast forward 13 years—armed with deep self-study of neuroscience, psychology, yoga, and rehabilitation medicine—I was ready to share my insights. Writing became a creative joy, an inspiring act of self-expression. Now, I know writing, particularly in self-help, is my calling: to offer others the book I once desperately needed.

How do you schedule your life when you're writing?

I stick to a morning routine like glue—early nights (no doomscrolling or wine!) mean I rise before dawn, refreshed and ready for two focused hours of writing magic. My day then rolls on as usual, juggling doctoring, parenting, cooking, and life. Occasionally, I escape for a luxurious, undisturbed week of writing and editing—pure bliss! Protecting this time is essential because, like most of us, I wear too many hats. Writing goals can only thrive when I create space for them, so I guard that time fiercely.

What would you say is your interesting writing quirk?

As a trained medical and scientific writer, I'm naturally precise and formal. But my personal voice loves sneaking through—my editor was shocked by an occasional swear word! Some got axed, but I kept a few gems for comedic timing or emotional punch. Balancing my professional persona and my authentic, relaxed self was a challenge, but I think readers will enjoy the realness. Writing should feel like a conversation, right? A little imperfection and humour make it relatable.

How did you get your book published?

I self-published through Amazon and IngramSpark after agents and publishers initially passed me by (low social media following—ouch!). Determined, I invested in two professional edits that elevated the book to a level I'm so proud of. Self-publishing was my best choice—why wait years to share Mastering Real Wellness? Still, my dream is to work with a publisher and agent to help spread the message far and wide. For now, between shifts as a doctor, I'm doing everything I can to get my book into readers' hands.

Where did you get your information or idea for your book?

Mastering Real Wellness was born from my unique blend of professional expertise and lived experience. I combined insights from medical science, neuroscience, psychology, yoga, and rehabilitation medicine to develop a simple, practical framework for thriving. The book shares skills I use daily—both for myself and my patients—alongside real-life case studies, takeaways, and a sprinkling of my personal journey. It's relatable, credible, and designed to help others navigate life's challenges and live optimally.

The Promise of Unbroken Straw
by Ken Steele

When did you first realize you wanted to be a writer?

I enjoyed writing from my earliest days in school, but my education/career took me down a different path. However, my engineering colleagues didn't take long to notice the other skill set. So early on, I was placed in assignments that showcased the other side of that coin, including speechwriting for senior executives. But to be clear, most of my professional career exercised the left side of my brain. Writing fed the other half, and I thoroughly enjoyed imagining a world I'd created, in this case, one that allowed me to reconnect with my adolescent self.

How do you schedule your life when writing?

I was fortunate that my day job was structured around a 9/80 schedule that offered me every other Friday off. Much of this novel was written during that and other downtime. Don't tell my employers, but a few words may have snuck onto the page at other times. And you'd think that retirement would afford more time, but alas, our schedule remains active. So, the novel's completion was shoe-horned around other things. Looking ahead, we'll see who wins the day, but if writing is the goal, I recommend against retiring in the mountains.

What would you say is your interesting writing quirk?

I'm slow as hell. It takes me dozens of tries to craft a single sentence, and upon rereads and edits, I realize I'm just getting started. So to borrow a metaphor from a different art form, the process for me is more like sculpting than painting. I've got to shave off a thousand fragments before something interesting emerges. Perhaps that reflects my lack of formal training, I'm not sure. But I do know this. Once things begin to take shape, I know exactly where I'm heading until, eventually, I make peace with that creation.

How did you get your book published?

Churchill got it right. "Never give in, never, never, never . . ." Writing is, by far, the hardest thing I've ever attempted, and I've tackled some pretty complex problems throughout my career. This project spanned 15 years (off and on), and there were numerous highs and lows, painfully close calls, and soul-crushing rejections. Two agents had represented me over that period but crossed the finish line alone. Eventually, I found an Indie publisher who believed in the work as much as I did, one who was located less than 2 miles from the house where I was born.

What did you get your idea for the book?

The novel, in part, commemorates the land where my ancestors had taken root. My father, and his father before him, lived on a wheat farm just prior to when this story takes place. I also wanted to weave my chosen profession into a storyline people could relate to. Finally, I wanted to give voice to people who are in pain, which is one of the underlying themes of this work.

The Koshertarian Comedians
by Michael Kornbluth

When did you first realize you wanted to be a writer?

I owe the vision of becoming a writer to my ex-girlfriend Erica. She saw something in me that I didn't know existed. I knew I was funny, but becoming a working writer in Hollywood one day was a heady possibility for me to contemplate at the time because my writing ego hadn't emerged yet. Still, getting staffed on a sitcom to write storylines for Curb or Family Guy versus cold calling IT Directors for a living became a worthy goal to shoot for at 24. I eventually started standup at 27 because I cold-called an alum from Ithaca who worked on Everyone Loves Raymond. I told him that I wanted to write sitcoms for a living. He said, "Do standup." So, I eventually did. For my 25th Birthday, Erica took me to a taping of Friends on the Warner Brothers lot. She pointed at the writers talking to the actors between takes, suggesting different lines to sample,e and said, "That could be you one day." What a move, what a remarkable woman. I loved making her sisters and mom laugh. I met Erica in Westwood, CA, after I started my 1st IT staffing job with Remington Intl. on Wilshire Blvd.

The Koshertarian Comedians

Michael Kornbluth

I only started writing TV spec scripts because of her. Erica was an executive assistant for a prominent lit agency at the time. The feedback on our 1st spec script was for Malcolm and the Middle. Yes, I'm older than Aids. The intended laughs in the script were almost non-existent, but I remember her lit agent boss commenting on how the writing was more dramatic. Still, he laughed at the line from the mother when mentioning how this is why they only use plastic silverware now. Standup comedians and comedy writers always remember the laughs.

How do you schedule your life when writing?

I hole myself up in our bedroom and bang away at the keyboard while listening to plenty of hair metal power ballads, Miles Davis, or from a specific playlist for my latest writing project, such as my screenplay in the making, The Gum King Of New York I drink generic Nespresso pods from Amazon, do some planks, morning prayer and meditation to get my brain flowing prior This past Sunday, I did a Google search on Jewish Angels because I wanted to mine material for a new bit about a City of Angels shirt that I bought at Pridemark I bought a shirt that says Los Angeles on the front, but what made me uncomfortable was the angel design on the back So, by purchasing the shirt I forced myself to delve into why a 48-year-old Jewish New Yorker, still got visibly tense over the prospect of advertising gentile angels on his back Now, I call this shirt my Judas shirt because I feel like I'm betraying my Jewish soul in it The Jewish guilt is what I deserve for advertising Gentile Angels on my back because deep down, I know that angel artwork has always been more of a Christian thing. Jews have two angels with major brand name recognition, Michael and Gabriel, and that's it.

06

Finding Color
by Candace MacPhie

How do you schedule your life when you're writing?

Sometimes, it's easy to procrastinate or find anything else to do except write. Then there are those times I get sucked in and spend hours crafting words into a story. This feast or famine leaves me disappointed I didn't write or exhausted when I spent too long doing it. So I set goals. Page goals, then review goals and set completion targets. It gives me the 'freedom' to be finished for the day when I've reached my goals; the work I do is focused and usually better content.

Where did you get your information or idea for your book?

My five-part Back in a Year series is based on an around-the-world backpacking trip I did in the '90s. I cracked open my journals and heavy photo albums, and from there, I created an adventure you're immersed in from page one to the last. I aim for the reader to feel the heat of the desert, the cold of Russia, and the emotions of traveling worldwide in taxis, buses, and trains. The readers will meet the people and experience the culture all in the frame of life in the '90s before cell phones and the Internet were at your fingertips.

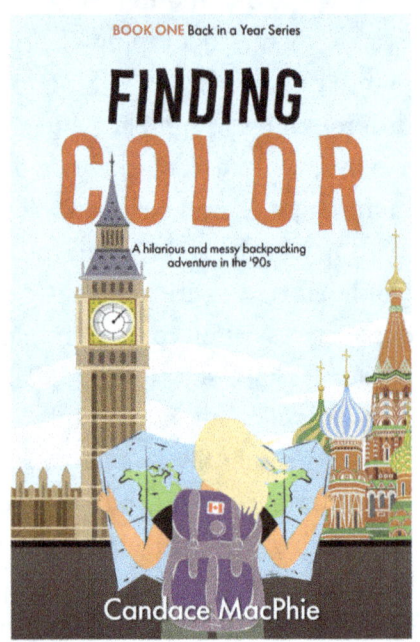

What was one of the most surprising thing you learned in creating your book?

I worked in the corporate world for twenty years, having some cool jobs and amazing teams. When I left that behind to take up writing full-time, I thought I would miss the buzz of the job—that inner satisfaction when solving a complex problem. But I found that in writing—the fulfillment of nailing a scene, finding the perfect word, or conjuring the right emotions. It was smaller in scope but still there.

What I missed most was the support people. They used to be a holler away and would help with any work concern I had. Writing is lonely. The most surprising part was people's unwavering support during my writing journey. Their generosity of time – if I asked for it. Meet for coffee to discuss a story arc or willingness to brainstorm book titles or cover art. Although we work in different places, my colleagues, friends, and family still cheer me on.

Callum Walker and the Fractured Veil by J. M. Shaw

When did you first realize you wanted to be a writer?

I started writing thirty-two years ago because I needed a creative outlet. I loved making up stories, and since my mother had just bought me a typewriter, I tried my hand at writing. If I had to pinpoint the moment when I wanted to become a writer, that day, sitting at the dining room table, picking at the keys one by one, was that moment.

However, what started as a hobby soon became a passion and, eventually, an obsession. Now, I write because it's entertaining, good stress relief, and emotional therapy all rolled into one, and I cannot imagine myself doing anything else.

How do you schedule your life when you're writing?

First and foremost, I am a wife and mother. My husband and I have two busy boys demanding much of our time and attention.

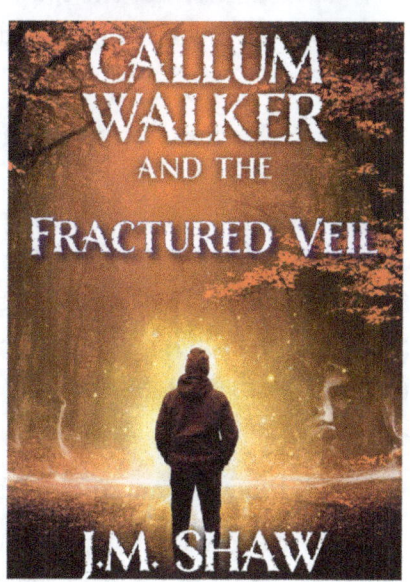

While I spend as much quality time with my family, when everyone else is occupied, I will stay with my laptop in a quiet corner of our house and write as much as possible until someone notices me. I usually get about twenty to thirty minutes of creative musing before my kids start fighting or demanding snacks. Most of my writing happens on weekdays when my husband works and my kids are at school. I will typically rush through the housework and errands in the first hour or two so that nothing is left waiting when I finally sit at my desk.

Because I have autism and ADHD, writing can quickly become hyperfocus. I must set the alarm before I begin because I have been known to spend several hours working without realizing the passage of time. Once my children and husband return home, I typically put away my writing for the rest of the evening. Occasionally, I will try to work after my sons go to bed, but I often choose to relax.

What would you say is your interesting writing quirk?

I am not a planner. I have a solid idea of the beginning and end of each novel and approximately what needs to happen in the middle, but the rest is undecided. I feel that this allows me the freedom to let my creative juices flow, and, at times, the story seems to write itself, and I'm just along for the ride. These moments of in-the-zone writing have often created scenes for which I receive the most compliments.

08

Something About Nobility by Jonni Jordyn

When did you first realize you wanted to be a writer?

I realized not only that I liked writing but that I had a talent for it while I was in college. I started writing in high school and enjoyed it, so I took as many creative writing classes in college as possible. Still, I also attended acting, music, sketching, and a handful of biology classes, but then I discovered I had a computer knack. This led me to a well-paying job in IT and left me having to select one of my other loves for my avocation, and I had some immediate opportunities in music. I played with stars from the 70s and performed on tours for legendary players. I left music after about twenty years and returned to writing, which I've been doing ever since. The Mother of All Viruses was the first book I wrote, but not the first I published.

How do you schedule your life when you're writing?

Currently, I do most of my writing in the morning before work. I plan to retire soon, so I may sleep later and write longer. If scheduling conflicts arise, I evaluate them by urgency before how important they are to me, but in a tie, my partner and family will come first. Sometimes, I'm deeply into a section and do not want to interrupt my flow, but sometimes, I must do something else. The ballet will not wait for me to arrive. I wrote The Mother of All Viruses while contracting out of my home state and had lots of spare time on weekends.

Where did you get your information or idea for your book?

Most of my ideas come from my neurodivergent imagination, but this book came from a computer program I wrote to simulate genetics. I designed an organism with two thousand genes spread across two chromosome pairs. Many of the principles used in the book relate directly back to the code I wrote. (It works, too.) I only had to add ways for it to become dangerous and then build some intrigue around it.

What do you like to do when you're not writing?

I used to keep busy with outdoor activities, such as skiing, bicycling, golf, etc. I also loved playing volleyball aggressively, but a high-speed bike crash destroyed one shoulder, and I had to give up volleyball. As the years catch up to me, I still plan to ski, but when the weather improves, I'll be hiking and exploring with my partner. I gave her an enormous deck of adventure cards with places to go.

Delicious Surrender by Luce Sutherland

When did you first realize you wanted to be a writer?

It started in my late twenties. After a long-term relationship ended, I started reading many juicy books, from Harlequins to historical romances and then the steamier kind in Black Lace novels. It was then that I knew I wanted to write my own. I took a night school course, but my consistency and commitment weren't there. For the next 20+ years, I dabbled and drafted stories, but writing was on the back burner while I focused on motherhood and my career. Until five years ago... when I decided it was now or never!

How do you schedule your life when you're writing?

When I started writing Delicious Surrender, the lockdowns had just begun, and I was working away from my family. Suddenly, I had much time alone in the evenings and during the weekends because travel and socializing were all but banned. I had always been a night owl, and it was in those quiet evenings that I rediscovered my creative side. I will always view that time as a gift.

Once we returned to normal, I continued to gravitate to my office after dinner most nights to continue what I'd started. Yes, I was missing all the incredible shows everyone else was watching on Netflix, but when those creative juices flowed, I could write all night or until the screen went blurry.

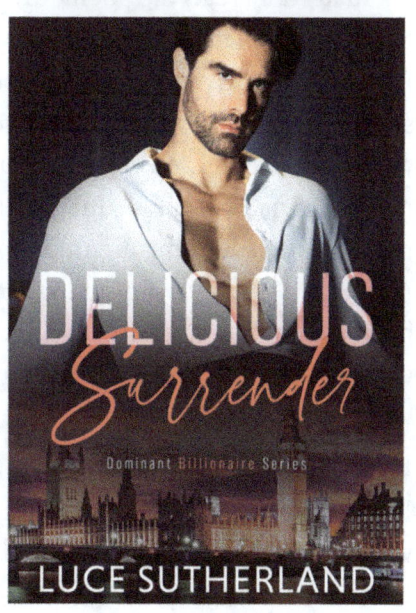

What would you say is your interesting writing quirk?

I have two quirks. The first is my need to eliminate distractions because I have several markers of ADD: hyperfocus and lack of focus. If I struggle with a particular scene, the slightest thing (sounds, emails, remembering I didn't pay a bill, or a flying bug in my office) will pull me out of my story. On the flip side, when I'm on a roll, I can ignore everything and everyone for hours on end.

When I'm immersed in the story, I go to sleep and wake up thinking about it. My family complains that I walk around in a fog. Another place where creative ideas flourish is during a massage. So, when I am writing completely, I book those as often as possible to reduce neck and shoulder stress and fill my well of inspiration.

How did you get your book published?

Sheer determination and impatience. After writing and editing for over two years, I started hunting for an agent. I spent an inordinate amount of time researching agencies and writing personalized query letters. I continued to polish the manuscript and grew progressively impatient to see my book come to life.

By June 2023, I was ready to take matters into my own hands. I found beta readers, hired a professional editor, started dreaming of technicolor covers, and found a book coach. The decision to self-publish felt right, and I never looked back. It's been a whirlwind since then, but I wouldn't change a thing.

Past Life's Revenge by Angela Van Breemen

When did you first realize you wanted to be a writer?

For me, this realization evolved in an organic way. I have been writing poetry from an early age. Poetry was a way of expressing how I perceived the world; it gave me the opportunity to articulate my feelings about family, school, and in particular, nature. Writing was such a natural evolution for me, that it never even occurred to me to call myself a writer, or even say, "I want to be a writer." It just happened.

My first experience with the power of words was when I was about ten. My parents were having an argument, an unusual occurrence in our household. I walked upstairs, sat at my writing desk and wrote a poem called "Dawn is Not Long Now." When I showed the poem to my mom and dad, they read the poem, drew me into their arms and like magic, the negativity had dissipated.

From then on, I wrote mainly poetry, although in my mid-twenties I started a novel, Past Life's Revenge, which I left uncompleted for many years. Several decades later, I found that old manuscript, assessed it, decided it had potential, and published it just last year. Publishing that novel was a redefining moment for me.

Although I have worn many hats over the years, from sales, to businesswoman, website and graphic designer to volunteering at a wildlife rescue, at this stage in my life, I am proud to say, "I am a writer."

How do you schedule your life when you're writing?

It certainly takes balance and discipline. I have a whole life: volunteering for Procyon Wildlife Rehabilitation and Education Centre, pursuing my love of music (a soprano soloist), and maintaining our large country property.

I want to say I devote time each day to writing, but other commitments and duties can interfere. Fortunately, it tends to be in waves whenever I write, and it's not unusual to write 3,000 words daily. However, even on the days I am not writing, I keep my iPhone close by so that I can immediately dictate any enhancements to the plot or characters. For me, inspiration can come at any time, whether it's a poem, an idea for the book I am currently working on, or a snippet of a melody for a song.

Getting the idea recorded is essential since I believe these bits of inspiration come from a higher source and should never be neglected or ignored.

Abella and the Haunted House by Zane Carson Carruth

Where did you get your information or idea for your book?

I pull many of my book ideas from my daily living activities. I write about something I can relate to or am going through. I wrote Abella Goes to the Rodeo because my husband was Chairman of the Board of the Houston Livestock Show and Rodeo, and I was First Lady of the Rodeo. I had front-row access to everyone and everything. This provided much material to work with. I wrote Abella and the Haunted House about a house in my neighborhood. Abella Gets a New Hairdo, and Abella and the Almost Racehorse came directly from my life experiences. I've found this makes for much richer content because I have invested emotionally in the life events and have lots of material to pull from.

What do you like to do when you're not writing?

When I am not writing, working out is usually on my mind. I don't like to sit for long periods, and writing requires a lot of quiet and stillness. Therefore, when time is available, I make a point of going to the gym or doing video exercise tapes at home. I love walking and will try to get the 10,000 recommended steps daily.

What was one of the most surprising thing you learned in creating your book?

I have learned that the mind is an incredible and powerful thing. It's our most fantastic organ and can produce magic when called upon. I have often thought, "How am I going to create this idea or get my idea across?" and learned that if I relax and let the imagination go, magic happens. The books write themselves.

How do you process and deal with negative book reviews?

It is a unique feeling to receive a negative book review. Be it just one sentence within the review or the entire review. I have received both. We should look at it as a badge of courage. It takes tremendous courage to display your passion for the whole of the world to see and judge. And judge, they do. Luckily, I received nothing but excellent reviews in my first several years. That boosted my confidence and encouraged my writing. One day, I received a scathing review. (Scathing!)I was pretty taken aback because I write children's books. How bad can a children's book about the tooth fairy be to get all worked up and write a scathing review? The review was not solicited; it was voluntarily submitted. The reviewer read every page and trashed every idea written. I would have just stopped reading the book if I hated it as severely as that person and not have written a very long, detailed negative review. However, that's what they did,d and I was stunned. After gathering my composure, I re-read it and thought I would try and learn from it as best as possible. I looked at the critical points made, wanted to see it from their point of view, gave them credit where I could, and dismissed the rest as someone in a rotten mood.

TARDY TECHNOLOGY: THE CURIOUS CASE OF SCIENCE FICTION'S SLOW BIRTH

Brad C. Anderson

We have told tales since we developed language to speak. Our early stories were sagas of heroism, mythology, and bawdy chronicles of sordid affairs. Modern-day librarians could easily categorize these ancient tales into adventure, fantasy, romance, etc. Yet, one modern-day genre seems conspicuously absent among the stories shared through most of human history: science fiction.

The first glimpse of something resembling science fiction appeared in True History by Lucien of Samosata in the second century AD. But the genre didn't stick. It was fourteen hundred years before Johannes Kepler wrote Somnium in 1634, describing a fantastical journey to the moon. Still, the genre failed to take hold until 1818, when Mary Shelley wrote Frankenstein, or The Modern Prometheus, after which science fiction took off. Why was science fiction such a latecomer? Did ancient people not dream of the future? To answer this, let's look at why we tell stories.

As described in A Narrative Approach to Organization Studies, through stories, we process complexity, helping us understand war, relationships, and an array of other overwhelming topics. Importantly, stories help a society vicariously process its hopes and fears over scary issues of the day.

What's this got to do with science fiction's tardiness?

I suspect that, for most of human history, technological advancement was so slow that it rarely intruded on people's lives. The technological world you were born into was the same as the one you died in, and that world was probably recognizable to your parents and children. When ancient people imagined the future, they likely imagined a world much like their present. When advancement takes generations, science fiction is simply fiction.

The Enlightenment changed all that. Technology's speed increased. The world you died in looked very different from the one in which you were born. The future became something with which we must contend. And thus, science fiction was born to help us process these bewildering changes.

From the optimism of Star Trek to the despair of Warhammer 40K, science fiction primes us to engage with technological advancement. Science fiction was late to the party because, for most of human history, we did not need it. But today, as we live through multiple world-changing technological revolutions, science fiction has never been more important.

OVERCOMING THE TRIBAL MIND
Don Sawyer

My latest book, The Burning Gem, is premised on the idea that we have not evolved fast enough to overcome our tribal constraints and collectively address the existential challenges that threaten our survival. In the book, a shadowy cabal committed to implementing Nietzsche's rule of the Übermensch uses sorcery and magic to promote its ends. But if you hold the magic (except for AI, social media, virtual reality, etc.), how far-fetched is this concept?

The nature of a tribe is that your identity depends on a standard set of beliefs, attitudes, and behaviors. A tribe shares a mythology that idealizes their nobility, gallantry, and chivalry and is often a rigidly constructed religion that is likely to crack if questioned. Loyalties are to a narrow circle of tribespeople whose worldview is molded by isolation, fear of the Other, and a deeply ingrained sense of victimhood and constant threat from outside forces of change.

And the point is they are right. Those of us who have moved on with the tide of modernity DO want to change our way of life. Their way of life is anathema to a sustainable world, a just and inclusive society, and a commitment to policies based on fact and science rather than superstition.

But it's not easy. As George Lakoff puts it, "We cannot think just anything — only what our embodied brains permit." Changing what the "brain permits" is at the core of our fight for a new global identity and abandoning evolutionary distrust of those who do not look, act, speak, or think like "us."

The Burning Gem asks, "Who benefits from maintaining tribal divisions, sowing fears that keep us apart, generating chaos and wars, hopelessness?" and then offers the only solution—the oligarch's rule.

The book and its sequel, The Tunnels of Buda, are metaphorical responses to this existential threat. A group of individuals draws on different personal and cultural backgrounds to fight against the shadowy forces that promote discord, an ancient cabal located deep underground and in our unconscious minds.

EMBRACING A SEASON OF RESTORATION: REIGNITING YOUR PASSION AS A WRITER

Dr. Katherine Hutchinson-Hayes

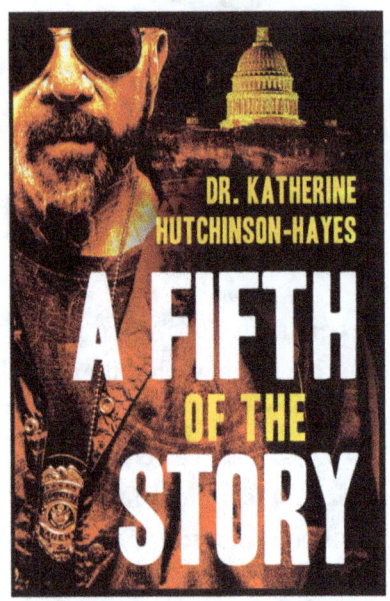

Writers often experience feelings of inadequacy and self-doubt. There were times I questioned my talent and determination to achieve my goals. Yet, limitations do not define me; our aspirations can exceed our fears and uncertainties.

I remember a discouraging time when I received rejection letters and imposter syndrome. I considered leaving writing for a conventional career. However, through persistence, I rediscovered my passion. Unexpected opportunities emerged—public speaking, published articles, and deep connections with readers. This change stemmed not only from my efforts but also from the support I received along the way.

Through these experiences, I realized that this journey isn't only about talent; it's about embracing the potential for renewal and growth. I found more significant rewards in navigating these ups and downs, like the promise of overcoming difficulties and finding new paths forward.

Three Ways to Reignite Your Passion as a Writer

1. Revitalize Your Purpose

When writing feels aimless, it's a chance to rediscover its meaning. Reconnecting with your vision can infuse your work with inspiration. I realized my words can impact others and create connections, reigniting my passion for writing.

2. Restore Your Confidence

Embrace the idea that you don't need to be perfect to succeed; your unique voice and perspective are what truly matter. Allow yourself to step into your role as a writer with renewed confidence.

3. Rekindle Your Joy

When self-doubt clouds creativity, focus on what brings joy in writing. Celebrating small victories can shift your mindset from doubt to gratitude and excitement for your journey.

Have you experienced any shifts in your writing journey lately? Take a moment to reflect on aspects of your creative process that could benefit from a fresh perspective.

1. Identify three areas in your writing for improvement or inspiration.

2. Reflect on how to revitalize your creativity in those areas.

3. Share your thoughts with a fellow writer or someone needing a creative boost.

Let's embrace this chance for renewal, believing the possibilities ahead are endless.

WATERCOLORS AND TEARS BY JOSÉ ORLANDO CASTAÑEDA

Manuel, a young Ecuadorian, sells medicinal herbs in the market and paints watercolors in his spare time. In search of a better life, he emigrates to Port Chester (New York). Elvira, his wife, intends to join him by sea, but she is shipwrecked. Her plans change after her rescue, and she ends up in Madrid, where she is employed as a nanny. Antonio, the father of the children in her care, discovers her secretly reading a novel from his antique books collection. He slyly labels a passage with a strip of paper, intending for her to read it. Intrigued, Elvira responds by indicating her own phrases in the book. That's the beginning of an innocent exchange of literary quotes through which love quietly slips in. While Manuel takes refuge in his paintings and herbal remedies on the other side of the world, Elvira finds herself falling for Antonio. When her hopes are dashed through a casual blunder, she seeks to regain her marital home and travels to Port Chester to be with her husband. Confronted by an unexpected tragedy, she discovers the watercolors that Manuel has painted in his solitude. His brushstrokes cut deep into her heart.

TILL I BLEED NO MORE BY ALEXANDER ELLIS

'The maroons think I will have to choose between survival and revenge, but for me, revenge was survival. It is the survival of my soul, and without it, I might as well die here and now.'

It is 1728, and the age of piracy is now over. After being defeated in battle by pirate hunters, a survivor named Casper Nait is left stranded on an island. After surviving there Casper is reunited with the same hunters that almost killed him; and is now forced into a brutal battle for survival against them. Fuelled by the deaths of his captain and crew, Casper embarks on a dangerous quest for revenge, with one himself to rely upon in a new post-pirate world.